No Longer Property of
Anythink Libraries/
Rangeview Library District

D0603003

A Is for Albatross

ABCs of Endangered Birds

by Sharon Katz Cooper

Consultant: Sarena Randall Gill
Community Engagement Manager
Phoenix Zoo / Arizona Center for Nature Conservation

CAPSTONE PRESS
a capstone imprint

A+ Books are published by Capstone Press,
1710 Roe Crest Drive, North Mankato, Minnesota 56003
www.mycapstone.com

Copyright © 2017 by Capstone Press, a Capstone imprint. All rights reserved. No part of this publication may be reproduced in whole or in part, or stored in a retrieval system, or transmitted in any form or by any means, electronic, mechanical, photocopying, recording, or otherwise, without written permission of publisher.

Library of Congress Cataloging-in-Publication Data
Library of Congress Cataloging-in-Publication data is available on the Library of Congress website.
ISBN 978-1-4914-8032-8 (library binding)
ISBN 978-1-4914-8403-6 (eBook PDF)
Summary: Describes endangered birds of the world by assigning a species or bird-related term to each letter of the alphabet.

Editorial Credits:
Jill Kalz, editor; Bobbie Nuytten, designer; Jo Miller, media researcher;
Katy LaVigne, production specialist

Image Credits:
Minden Pictures: Martin Hale, 18, Otto Plantema, 7; Nature Picture Library: Tim Laman, 24; Newscom: Danita Delimont Photography/Larry Ditto, 20, Danita Delimont Photography/Maresa Pryer, 28, Design Pics, 17, Minden Pictures/BIA/Jacob S. Spendelow, 21, Minden Pictures/Michael Quinton, 8, Minden Pictures/Pete Oxford, 15, Minden Pictures/Steve Gettle, 14, Photoshot/NHPA/Hira Punjabi, 9, Photoshot/NHPA/Lee Dalton, 11, Photoshot/NHPA/Martin Wendler, 27; Shutterstock: antantarctic, 4, Atthapol Saita, cover (bottom middle), 5, Elnur, 29, Emi, 13, FloridaStock, 25, Giedriius, 22, Kent Ellington, 26, Robert L Kothenbeutel, cover (bottom left), 10, Steve Byland, 19, Steve Oehlenschlager, cover, (top), Steven Blandin, 1 (left), Tammy Venable, 6, zixian, 1 (right), 12; Wikimedia: Francesco Veronesi from Italy, 23, Jeol Trick of the U.S. Fish and Wildlife Service Headquarters, cover (bottom right), R. Kohley of U.S. Fish & Wildlife Service - Pacific Region, 16

Design Elements:
Shutterstock: Ramona Heim, vadimmmus

Printed and bound in the USA.
009690F16

Note to Parents, Teachers, and Librarians

The E for Endangered series supports national science standards related to zoology. This book describes and illustrates birds. The images support early readers in understanding the text. The repetition of words and phrases helps early readers learn new words. This book also introduces early readers to subject-specific vocabulary words, which are defined in the Glossary section. Early readers may need assistance to read some words and to use the Share the Facts, Glossary, Internet Sites, Critical Thinking Using the Common Core, Read More, and Index sections of the book.

ENDANGERED!

Endangered plants and animals are at high risk of disappearing. Our planet may lose them forever because of habitat loss, hunting, or other threats. When one species goes away, the loss often hurts other species. All life on Earth is connected in some way.

All of the birds in this book are in trouble. They are either near threatened (at some risk), vulnerable (at more risk), or endangered. Their numbers are small. But they don't have to disappear. You can help by reading more about them and sharing what you learn with others.

Aa:
albatross

Albatross are large birds with webbed feet. They have the largest wingspan of any bird. The wingspan of the endangered Tristan albatross may reach 11 feet (3.4 meters). Albatross can glide on the wind for hours without flapping their wings. They live near the ocean and eat fish and squid.

Bb:
blue-throated macaw

Blue-throated macaws live in a small part of Bolivia, a country in South America. They make their homes in palm trees. They eat seeds, berries, nuts, and fruits with their strong, hooked beaks. Blue-throated macaws are very rare. For many years poachers captured the colorful birds and sold them as pets around the world.

Cc: California condor

California condors are the largest flying birds in North America. They can glide 15,000 feet (4,572 m) above the ground. Condors eat meat, but they don't hunt. They eat dead animals. In the 1970s condors nearly went extinct. Many conservation groups worked to help them produce chicks in zoos. Some of those birds were released into the wild.

Dd:
duck

Laysan ducks get their name from the island on which they live—Laysan Island, in Hawaii. Although they can fly, they often don't. They usually walk or run instead. Laysan ducks hide during the day and feed at night. They eat mostly insects, especially brine flies. To catch brine flies, the ducks run through thick clouds of them with their bills open.

Ee:
emperor goose

Emperor geese live on the frozen land in the Arctic or along rocky shorelines. They stay close to salt water year-round. Emperor geese lay eggs along the coasts of Alaska and Siberia. In spring the birds eat roots. In summer they eat plants. In winter they eat clams and mussels.

Ff:
falcon

Red-headed falcons are small, quick birds. They live in South Asia, mostly in open areas with patchy trees. They hunt other small birds, such as sparrows. They also eat bats and insects. Red-headed falcons often hunt in pairs, scaring prey out from the trees.

Gg:
greater prairie-chicken

In the 1800s more than 14 million greater prairie-chickens lived in the western United States. By the 1900s, nearly all of them had disappeared. They were hunted, and their habitats were destroyed. People collected too many of their eggs. Most of today's vulnerable greater prairie-chickens live in the grasslands of Nebraska and South Dakota.

Hh:
habitat loss

Habitat loss is a big reason why birds become endangered. When people clear land to farm or to build roads and cities, birds can no longer live in those places. Birds cannot always move to new places. The new places may not have what the birds need. The birds may be forced to compete for food with animals already living there.

Ii:
i'iwi (ee-EE-vee)

I'iwis are also called scarlet Hawaiian honeycreepers. They have a red body with black wings. They use their long, curved bill to sip nectar from flowers. Like hummingbirds, they hover in mid-air.

Jj:
Japanese crane

Japanese cranes are the largest cranes in the world. Their wingspan measures about 8 feet (2.5 m). They are also called red-crowned cranes. They have a red patch of skin on their head. Japanese cranes eat both plants and small animals, such as fish. Only about 2,200 live in the wild.

Kk:
Kirtland's warbler

Kirtland's warblers live in the pine and oak forests of Michigan. They eat blueberries and insects. Forest fires are a big danger to this near-threatened species. So are brown-headed cowbirds. The cowbird lays its eggs in a warbler's nest. The cowbird chick hatches first and often takes all the food. Warbler chicks then have nothing to eat.

Ll:
Lear's macaw

Lear's macaws are large, colorful parrots from Brazil, a country in South America. They nest on cliffs and ledges. Lear's macaws get their name from Edward Lear. He was an artist in the 1800s. He liked to paint macaws. Macaws are popular birds for poachers to catch and sell as pets. One macaw may sell for thousands of dollars.

Mm:
millerbird

Millerbirds are tiny songbirds. They get their name from their favorite food: the miller moth. Millerbirds live only on the small island of Nihoa, in Hawaii. They build nests made of grass and roots in small bushes. They spend much of their time on the ground, looking for insects.

Nn:
nēnē (NAY-NAY)

Also known as Hawaiian geese, nēnēs are Hawaii's state bird. They make a low call that sounds like "nay nay." They used to live on all of the major Hawaiian islands. Today nēnēs are found only on Maui, Kauai, and the island of Hawaii. Dangers include habitat loss and predators such as mongooses, cats, and pigs.

Oo:
Oriental white stork

Oriental white storks live in the wetlands of China and eastern Russia. They stand nearly 4 feet (1.2 m) tall on long, red legs. They pluck fish, frogs, and other small prey from the water with their long bills. Unlike most birds, storks can't make sounds. They talk to each other by clicking their bills.

Pp:
piping plover

Piping plovers are small shorebirds. They live on sand dunes and coastal beaches. Female piping plovers lay three or four eggs in shallow holes. They then fill the holes with light colored stones and shells to hide the eggs. Once the chicks hatch, both parents feed them until they can fly—about 30 days later.

Qq:
quail

The calls of masked bobwhite quail sound like "bob-bob-white" or "ka-lo-kee." The birds are very rare. A small number of them live in southern Arizona and the Sonoran Desert. Forty years ago people feared that the birds had become extinct. Drought and overgrazing by cattle destroyed much of the quails' habitat.

Rr:
red-cockaded woodpecker

Red-cockaded woodpeckers get their name from the red feathers behind their eyes. They live only in a special kind of pine forest. These pine forests grow north from Florida to Virginia, and west to Oklahoma and eastern Texas. Deforestation is shrinking the pine forests and destroying the woodpeckers' habitat.

Ss:
Southern rockhopper penguin

Southern rockhopper penguins are the world's smallest penguins. Rather than waddle like other penguins, they hop! They live on islands near New Zealand and the southern tip of South America. They spend most of their time in shallow water. But they can dive as deep as 330 feet (101 m).

Tt:
Thyolo alethe
(thy-OH-loh AL-eh-thee)

Thyolo alethes are tiny birds with a soft, lovely song. They live in Malawi and Mozambique, countries in East Africa. Their name comes from the Malawi town of Thyolo. The birds follow swarms of marching ants. They feed on beetles and other insects stirred up by the ants.

Uu:
ultramarine lorikeet

Ultramarine lorikeets are noisy little birds. They have bright blue feathers and orange bills. They are found only on the Marquesas Islands, in the South Pacific Ocean. There they nest in trees and feed on fruit, especially mangos. They also feed on nectar from coconut palm and banana tree flowers.

Vv: Victory

Sometimes conservation groups bring an endangered species back from the edge of extinction. The American bald eagle is an example of a victory. It was endangered for many years. Poisons weakened eagle eggshells, killing chicks before they could hatch. Hunters shot many birds for sport. New laws and programs helped bald eagle numbers grow. They are no longer endangered.

Ww:
whooping crane

Whooping cranes are the tallest North American birds. They live in family groups around lakes and marshes. They eat fish, frogs, insects, and plants. At one time there were thousands of whooping cranes in the wild. By 1941 there were only 21 left. Habitat loss and hunting nearly made the cranes extinct.

Xx:
exotic pet trade

Some birds are endangered because people capture them to sell as pets. This is against the law in most places, but it happens often. Illegal hunters make a lot of money—billions of dollars each year. Conservation groups work hard to teach people that selling and buying endangered species as pets is wrong. They push for tougher laws.

Yy:
yellow-shouldered blackbird

Yellow-shouldered blackbirds live in coastal areas of Puerto Rico. They are found mostly in mangrove forests. Local people call them *mariquitas*, which means "ladybirds." They eat moths, crickets, seeds, and nectar. Male blackbirds will often form mobs to protect females and their eggs from predators.

Zz: zoo

Many zoos around the world keep flocks of at-risk birds and help them produce chicks. Some of the young birds may one day return to the wild. Zoos also teach visitors about at-risk birds. They give them ways to help.

SHARE THE FACTS

- The U.S. Fish and Wildlife Service estimates that as many as 91 species of birds are nearing extinction in the United States.

- Only about 250 blue-throated macaws remain in the wild.

- Operation Migration is a program that teaches young whooping cranes how to migrate for the first time by following a tiny airplane.

- Whooping cranes are able to fly 500 miles (805 kilometers) a day at 40 miles (64 km) per hour.

- The largest bald eagle nest found so far measured 10 feet (3 m) across and 20 feet (6 m) deep.

- In the 1950s only 412 nesting pairs of bald eagles remained. Now there are nearly 10,000.

- Male Japanese cranes do beautiful dances when they are trying to find a female. Once they do, they stay with the same mate for life.

- Pesticides are a great danger to birds. The poisons end up in the birds' food and make their eggs weak and unable to grow properly.

- The Great Backyard Bird Count is a free annual event held around the world. On one or more days of the four-day event, bird watchers of all ages spend 15 minutes counting the birds they see. The event helps researchers learn how well birds are doing. See www.audubon.org for more details.

- Some organizations that help protect birds in North America include **Partners in Flight** (*www.partnersinflight.org*), **American Bird Conservancy** (*abcbirds.org*), **National Audubon Society** (*www.audubon.org*), and **The Nature Conservancy** (*www.nature.org*).

GLOSSARY

conservation—the protection of plants, animals, and natural resources such as water and soil

deforestation—cutting down trees until a forest is destroyed

endangered—at risk of disappearing forever

extinct—when a species no longer exists on Earth

habitat—a place where an animal can find its food, water, shelter, and space to live

migrate—to move from place to place in different times of the year

near threatened—could become endangered in the near future

nectar—a sweet liquid found in many flowers

pesticide—a chemical that controls unwanted plants and animals

poacher—a person who hunts illegally

predator—an animal that hunts and eats other animals

protect—to save from danger

species—a group of plants or animals that share common traits

vulnerable—at high risk of becoming endangered

wingspan—the distance between the tips of a pair of wings when fully open

INTERNET SITES

FactHound offers a safe, fun way to find Internet sites related to this book. All of the sites on FactHound have been researched by our staff.

Here's all you do:

Visit *www.facthound.com*

Type in this code: 9781491480328

Check out projects, games and lots more at
www.capstonekids.com

CRITICAL THINKING USING THE COMMON CORE

1. Name three reasons why a bird species may become endangered. (Key Ideas and Details)

2. Use the photo on page 4 to explain what wingspan is. (Craft and Structure)

3. Explain how brown-headed cowbirds are a danger to the survival of Kirtland's warblers. (Key Ideas and Details)

READ MORE

Alderfer, Jonathan. *National Geographic Kids Bird Guide of North America: The Best Birding Book for Kids from National Geographic's Bird Experts.* Washington, D.C.: National Geographic, 2013.

Boothroyd, Jennifer. *Endangered and Extinct Birds.* Animals in Danger. Minneapolis: Lerner Publications Company, 2014.

Gagne, Tammy. *The Most Endangered Animals in the World.* All About Animals. North Mankato, Minn.: Capstone Press, 2015.

INDEX